INDIANAPOLIS
COLTS

BY TODD KORTEMEIER

SportsZone

An Imprint of Abdo Publishing
abdopublishing.com

abdopublishing.com

Published by Abdo Publishing, a division of ABDO, PO Box 398166, Minneapolis, Minnesota
55439. Copyright © 2017 by Abdo Consulting Group, Inc. International copyrights reserved in all
countries. No part of this book may be reproduced in any form without written permission from
the publisher. SportsZone™ is a trademark and logo of Abdo Publishing.

Printed in the United States of America, North Mankato, Minnesota
042016
092016

Cover Photo: Paul Jasienski/AP Images
Interior Photos: Paul Jasienski/AP Images, 1; Rusty Kennedy/AP Images, 4-5; David J. Phillip/
AP Images, 6; Chris Carlson/AP Images, 7; AP Images, 8-9; NFL Photos/AP Images, 10-11, 16-17;
Horace Cort/AP Images, 12-13; Vernon Biever/AP Images, 14-15; Al Messerschmidt/AP Images,
18-19, 24-25, 27; Bill Kostroun/AP Images, 20-21; Keith Srakocic/AP Images, 22-23; Scott Boehm/
AP Images, 26, 28-29

Editor: Patrick Donnelly
Series Designer: Nikki Farinella

Cataloging-in-Publication Data
Names: Kortemeier, Todd, author.
Title: Indianapolis Colts / by Todd Kortemeier.
Description: Minneapolis, MN : Abdo Publishing, [2017] | Series: NFL up close |
    Includes index.
Identifiers: LCCN 2015960433 | ISBN 9781680782196 (lib. bdg.) |
    ISBN 9781680776300 (ebook)
Subjects: LCSH: Indianapolis Colts (Football team)--History--Juvenile
    literature. | National Football League--Juvenile literature. | Football--Juvenile
    literature. | Professional sports--Juvenile literature. | Football teams--
    Indiana--Juvenile literature.
Classification: DDC 796.332--dc23
LC record available at http://lccn.loc.gov/201596043

TABLE OF CONTENTS

A TITLE FOR INDY 4

THE NEW COLTS 8

NEAR MISSES AND A TITLE 12

BYE-BYE BALTIMORE 16

ANOTHER SLOW START 20

FROM MANNING TO LUCK 24

Timeline 30
Glossary 31
Index / About the Author 32

A TITLE FOR INDY

The early 2000s was a good time for the Indianapolis Colts. With Peyton Manning at quarterback, they were one of the best teams in the National Football League (NFL). But they started to become known more for their near misses than their success. Manning and the Colts won their division five times. But they had yet to make it to the Super Bowl.

That changed in 2006. The Colts cruised to a 12-4 record and rolled into the Super Bowl as a heavy favorite against the Chicago Bears.

Peyton Manning, *18*, finally got the Indianapolis Colts to the Super Bowl after the 2006 season.

But the Colts got started on the wrong foot. Chicago's Devin Hester returned the opening kickoff for a touchdown. Manning then threw an interception, and Indianapolis trailed 14-6 after the first quarter.

It was all Colts after that. Manning and the offense chipped away at the Bears' defense. They took the lead midway through the second quarter and never looked back. Manning completed 25 of 38 passes for 247 yards and a touchdown. The Colts won 29-17, and Manning was named the Super Bowl Most Valuable Player (MVP). It was the first championship for the Colts since they moved to Indianapolis in 1984.

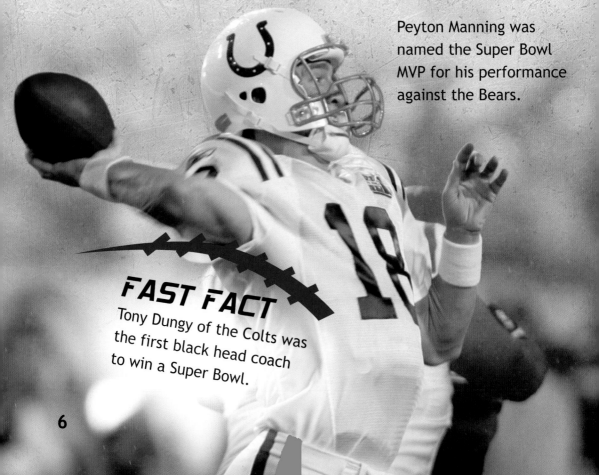

Peyton Manning was named the Super Bowl MVP for his performance against the Bears.

FAST FACT
Tony Dungy of the Colts was the first black head coach to win a Super Bowl.

Tony Dungy, *right*, cheers as Colts safety Bob Sanders returns an interception against the Chicago Bears in the Super Bowl.

The Colts were not very good in their early years, but it was not long before the rest of the NFL had its hands full trying to stop them.

THE NEW COLTS

The Colts began playing in Baltimore in 1953. They used the name of a previous team that folded in 1950. It was a fitting name for a team playing in Baltimore, a city with a long tradition of horse breeding and racing.

The new Colts struggled in their early years. Then a quarterback named Johnny Unitas arrived in 1955. As a rookie, Unitas had been cut by the Pittsburgh Steelers. The Colts picked him up the next season. They would not regret that decision.

FAST FACT

Memorial Stadium opened for the Colts' first season in 1953. It was their only home while in Baltimore.

The 1958 title game was the first overtime game in NFL history. It is often referred to as "The Greatest Game Ever Played."

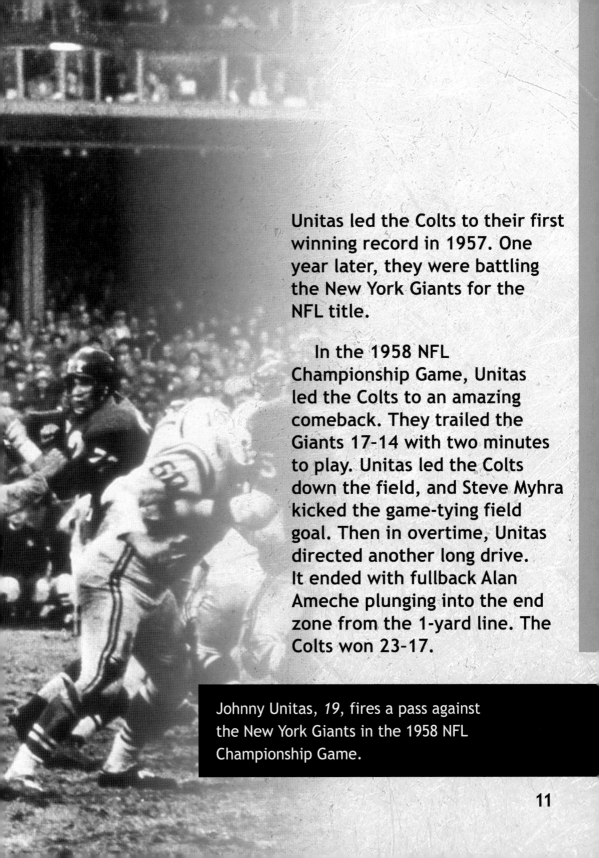

Unitas led the Colts to their first winning record in 1957. One year later, they were battling the New York Giants for the NFL title.

In the 1958 NFL Championship Game, Unitas led the Colts to an amazing comeback. They trailed the Giants 17-14 with two minutes to play. Unitas led the Colts down the field, and Steve Myhra kicked the game-tying field goal. Then in overtime, Unitas directed another long drive. It ended with fullback Alan Ameche plunging into the end zone from the 1-yard line. The Colts won 23-17.

Johnny Unitas, *19*, fires a pass against the New York Giants in the 1958 NFL Championship Game.

FAST FACT

Colts running back Lenny Moore set an NFL single-season record by scoring 20 touchdowns in 1964.

Lenny Moore was one of many stars in the Colts' lineup during their glory days in Baltimore.

NEAR MISSES AND A TITLE

Coach Weeb Ewbank led the Colts to a second straight championship in 1959. In 1963, Ewbank left Baltimore to coach the New York Jets in the rival American Football League (AFL).

Don Shula took over for Ewbank, and the future Hall of Famer made the Colts even better. They were known for their explosive offense. Johnny Unitas got plenty of help from his talented teammates, including wide receiver Raymond Berry, running back Lenny Moore, and tight end John Mackey. All three were future Hall of Famers.

In 1968, the Colts went 13-1. They had a punishing defense led by linebacker Mike Curtis, defensive end Bubba Smith, and cornerback Bobby Boyd. They made it to the Super Bowl, where they faced their former coach, Ewbank, and the AFL champion Jets. In one of the biggest upsets in NFL history, the Jets beat the Colts 16-7.

Shula left after the 1969 season. But the Colts stayed hot and made it back to the Super Bowl in 1970. They were tied with the Dallas Cowboys 13-13 as time was running out. Curtis intercepted a pass in Dallas territory. With nine seconds left, rookie kicker Jim O'Brien made a field goal, and the Colts won 16-13.

FAST FACT

Don Shula went on to coach the Miami Dolphins and won two Super Bowls. His 347 career victories are the most in NFL history.

Baltimore's pass rushers, including Bubba Smith, *78*, could not stop Joe Namath and the New York Jets in the Super Bowl.

BYE-BYE BALTIMORE

The Colts traded Johnny Unitas to the San Diego Chargers in 1973. That represented the end of the great championship Colts teams. Running back Lydell Mitchell became the focus of Baltimore's offense. He posted the first 1,000-yard rushing season in team history in 1975. The Colts won the division that year and the next two years after. But they lost in their first playoff game each time.

FAST FACT

Johnny Unitas played 17 years with the Colts. He threw for nearly 40,000 yards and 287 touchdowns. He was inducted into the Pro Football Hall of Fame in 1979.

Lydell Mitchell makes a cut against the Los Angeles Rams in a 1975 game at the Los Angeles Coliseum.

By the 1980s, the Colts had fallen on hard times. They went 2-14 in 1981. The next year they were 0-8-1 in a strike-shortened season. Off the field, the scene was even worse. Attendance was low. Memorial Stadium was aging. But nobody wanted to spend money to build a new stadium.

Faced with these problems, Colts owner Robert Irsay decided to move the team. In the early morning hours of March 29, 1984, moving vans were packed, and the Colts hit the road to Indiana.

Johnny Unitas waves to the crowd as he is honored at Memorial Stadium on October 9, 1977.

18

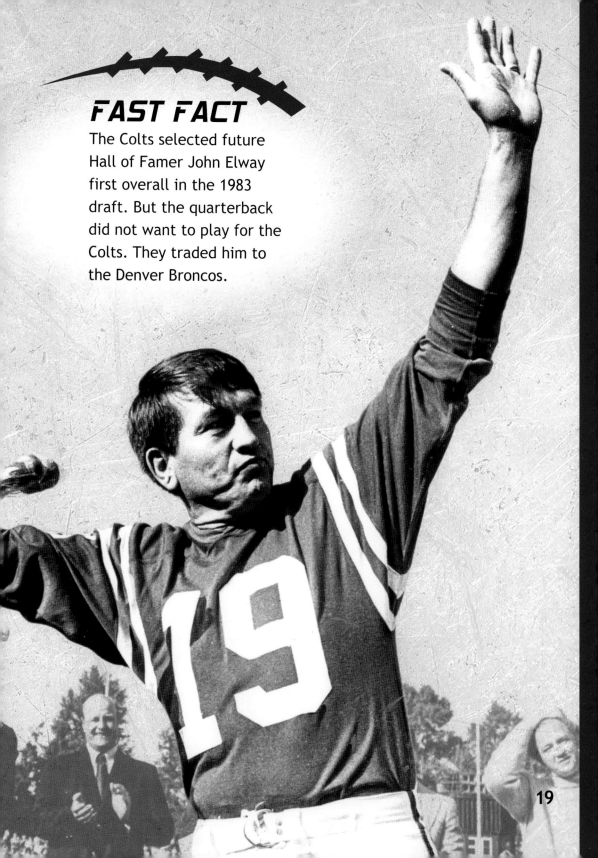

FAST FACT

The Colts selected future Hall of Famer John Elway first overall in the 1983 draft. But the quarterback did not want to play for the Colts. They traded him to the Denver Broncos.

ANOTHER SLOW START

The Colts did not find success right away in their new home. But in their fourth season, they made the playoffs. They did it with the help of running back Eric Dickerson, who won the NFL rushing title in 1988.

FAST FACT

The Colts acquired Eric Dickerson from the Los Angeles Rams in 1987. Indianapolis gave up six high draft picks and three players to get the star running back.

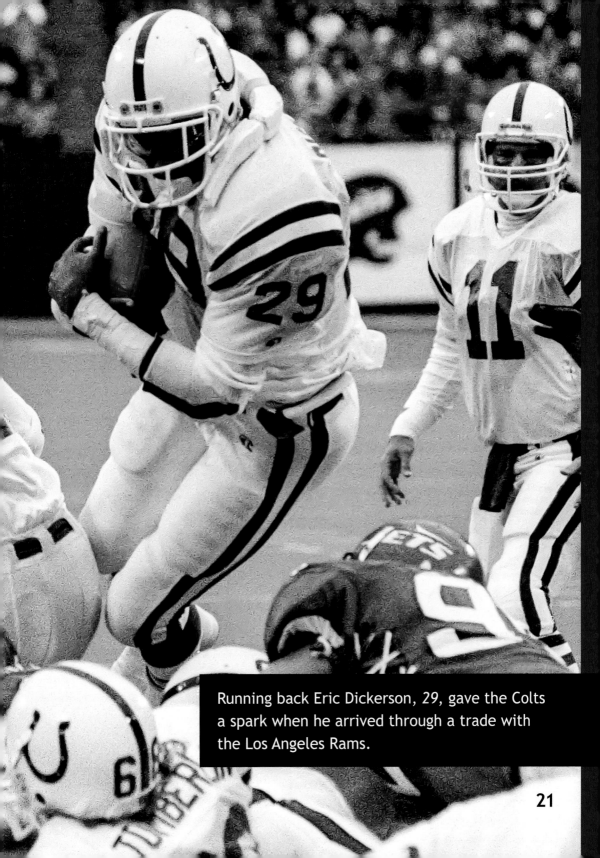

Running back Eric Dickerson, 29, gave the Colts a spark when he arrived through a trade with the Los Angeles Rams.

That playoff appearance was the only one in the Colts' first 11 seasons in Indianapolis. In 1994, the team drafted running back Marshall Faulk. Faulk was a great runner, but he also could catch passes. The Colts made it all the way to the conference championship in 1995. The game with the Pittsburgh Steelers came down to the final play. Colts quarterback Jim Harbaugh threw a desperation pass into the end zone. The ball bounced through a crowd of players and fell incomplete.

After another playoff appearance in 1996, Indianapolis finished 3-13 in 1997. That set the Colts up with the number one pick in the 1998 NFL Draft.

Colts wide receiver Aaron Bailey, *80*, can not hang on to Jim Harbaugh's last-gasp pass against the Pittsburgh Steelers.

FROM MANNING TO LUCK

Two great college quarterbacks entered the 1998 NFL Draft. The Colts had to decide who to take with the first pick. Expert opinions were split. Some liked Tennessee's Peyton Manning. Others preferred Ryan Leaf from Washington State.

The Colts went with Manning. It turned out to be the right call. Leaf's career was a big disappointment. Manning became one of the best quarterbacks in NFL history.

Peyton Manning, *right*, poses with NFL commissioner Paul Tagliabue at the 1998 NFL Draft.

The Colts only missed the playoffs twice with Manning as the starter. They made two Super Bowls and won one. Wide receiver Marvin Harrison led the league in receiving yards twice and retired with almost 15,000 career yards, all with the Colts. Linebacker Dwight Freeney, who was named to seven Pro Bowls, anchored the defense.

Dwight Freeney, 93, was a first-team All-Pro selection in 2004, 2005, and 2009.

Marvin Harrison had more than 1,100 receiving yards in eight straight seasons (1999-2006).

Manning missed the entire 2011 season with a neck injury. The Colts suffered without him. But their 2-14 record earned them the number one pick in the draft again. So they released Manning and took quarterback Andrew Luck.

Luck was their starter from the first day of his rookie training camp. He led the Colts to the playoffs each of his first three seasons. Luck appears to be the latest in a long line of championship Colts quarterbacks.

From Johnny Unitas to Peyton Manning to Andrew Luck, *12*, the Colts have often had great players at quarterback.

TIMELINE

1953
The Colts play their first season in Baltimore.

1956
The Colts sign future Hall of Fame quarterback Johnny Unitas.

1958
The Colts win their first NFL title in "The Greatest Game Ever Played."

1959
The Colts repeat as NFL champions.

1971
The Colts beat the Dallas Cowboys 16-13 on January 17 to win their first Super Bowl.

1984
The Colts move from Baltimore to Indianapolis.

1998
The Colts select quarterback Peyton Manning first in the draft.

2007
The Colts win their second Super Bowl, 29-17 over the Chicago Bears, on February 4.

2012
The Colts select quarterback Andrew Luck first in the draft.

GLOSSARY

CONFERENCE
A group of divisions that help form a league.

CUT
When a player is removed from a team's roster.

DEFENSIVE END
A player whose primary job is to get to the quarterback.

DIVISION
A group of teams that help form a league.

DRAFT
The process by which teams select players who are new to the league.

FULLBACK
An offensive player who sometimes runs with the football but is also responsible for blocking.

PLAYOFFS
A set of games played after the regular season that decides which team will be the champion.

INDEX

Ameche, Alan, 11

Bailey, Aaron, 23
Berry, Raymond, 13
Boyd, Bobby, 14

Curtis, Mike, 14

Dickerson, Eric, 20, 21
Dungy, Tony, 6, 7

Elway, John, 19
Ewbank, Weeb, 13-14

Faulk, Marshall, 22
Freeney, Dwight, 26

Harbaugh, Jim, 22, 23
Harrison, Marvin, 26, 27
Hester, Devin, 6

Irsay, Robert, 18

Leaf, Ryan, 24
Luck, Andrew, 28

Mackey, John, 13
Manning, Peyton, 4, 6, 24, 25, 26, 28

Mitchell, Lydell, 16, 17
Moore, Lenny, 12, 13
Myhra, Steve, 11

Namath, Joe, 15

O'Brien, Jim, 14

Sanders, Bob, 7
Shula, Don, 13-14
Smith, Bubba, 14, 15

Tagliabue, Paul, 25

Unitas, Johnny, 9, 11, 13, 16, 18, 28

ABOUT THE AUTHOR

Todd Kortemeier has authored dozens of books for young people, primarily on sports topics. He is a graduate of the University of Minnesota's School of Journalism & Mass Communication and lives near Minneapolis with his wife.